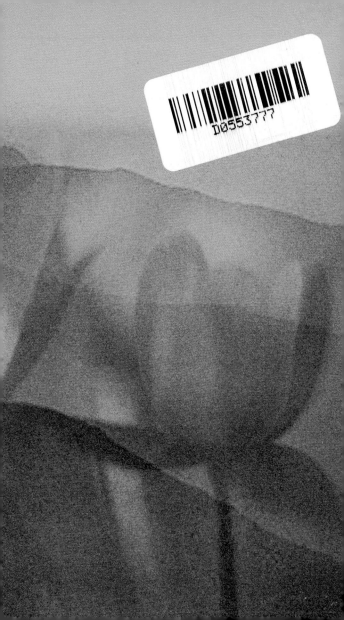

D0553777

Presented to

_____

By

_____

the *Miracle* of HEALING

PROMISES OF HEALING
FROM EVERY BOOK IN THE BIBLE

BENNY HINN

COUNTRYMAN

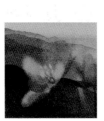

Do you believe in miracles?

Do they still happen today?

THESE TWO QUESTIONS are often asked of me, and I have discovered that there are varying opinions and perspectives regarding these questions among believers.

Most believers in the world today recognize and acknowledge that God has the power to heal, no matter what their denominational background may be. However, I have found that their perspective on *how* and *when* He heals differs greatly.

Some well-meaning individuals acknowledge that God did heal in what is often referred to as "the day of miracles"—a time when Jesus walked among men and lived on earth. But they go on to state with deep conviction that miracles are no longer possible because Jesus is not physically present on earth to perform the miraculous. As a result, they believe that divine healing has nothing to do with *today*.

Others will admit with reluctance that at times God may heal some needy individual. However, their perspective is based largely on a hope that God's mercy will somehow randomly fall on the needy, and an act of divine intervention will rescue them from certain tragedy and disaster.

Still others advocate a mind-over-matter approach, insisting that by maintaining a strong mental attitude, victory can be realized over sickness and adversity.

Throughout history, man has developed theories and philosophies about God, and has attempted to establish them as fact. But no matter what ideas or concepts man may contrive, one thing is certain: man's theories have no bearing upon God. God's attributes cannot be governed by man's ideas nor confined to man's timetables.

God's divine touch upon a broken body or mind is not merely a New Testament phenomenon from the days of the apostles and the Early Church. His ability to perform the miraculous is not and never has been restricted to a certain time frame in church history. God is no respecter of persons, for Hebrews 13:8 declares "Jesus Christ is the same, yesterday, today, and forever." Miracles still happen! And they are available to you and me!

God is a healing God, and His very presence births the hope of healing, deliverance, and restoration. Chronicled in every book of the Bible is God's power to heal. The Bible is the believer's handbook for living, and only through its sacred pages can we discover the nature and character of God, along with the benefits and blessings that belong to you and me as His children.

The Word of God is a Word of healing, and the promise of healing is found in every book of the Bible. The following pages contain a collection of verses on the topic of healing.

I have included at least one verse from every book of the Bible. If you or a loved one is in need of a miracle today, I encourage you to read each verse and meditate upon each promise. As you do, faith for the miraculous will be birthed within your heart to trust God for your every need.

BENNY HINN

SEPTEMBER 1998

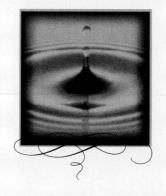

Promises
of Healing

from the
OLD TESTAMENT

God's healing is for your whole family.

So Abraham prayed to God; and God healed Abimelech, his wife, and his female servants. Then they bore children. . . .

GENESIS 20:17

God is the author of good health.

And they answered, "Your servant our father is in good health; he is still alive." And they bowed their heads down, and prostrated themselves.

GENESIS 43:28

God will counterattack the enemy's attack of affliction.

But as for you, you meant evil against me; but God meant it for good, in order to bring it about as it is this day, to save many people alive.

GENESIS 50:20

Benny Hinn

I TOLD A FELLOW MINISTER
in Florida recently, "I have to
believe in miracles. I have no
choice. With the sin and sickness
I see in our world, I doubt
I could face another day if I did
not believe that God can intervene
in the lives of man."

Because God heals, there is always
hope. Recently I spoke with the
father of a girl who was dying.
The moment he knew I was going
to pray for his daughter he said,
"You don't know what this means to
me. Now I can go to work today."
It was hope that gave him the
ability to go forward.

People continually ask me, "What
can I do to receive my miracle?"

"Nothing," I tell them.

Healing is not a result of what we
do. It is a result of what Christ
has *already done*.

THIS IS YOUR
DAY FOR A MIRACLE

The Miracle of Healing

God's presence will guide and direct you to walk in your healing through any trial, desert, or wilderness.

And the LORD went before them by day in a pillar of a cloud to lead the way, and by night in a pillar of fire to give them light; so as to go by day and night: He did not take away the pillar of cloud by day or the pillar of fire by night from before the people.

EXODUS 13:21–22

Let God fight your battle for you and defeat the attack of illness.

The LORD is my strength and song, and He has become my salvation [healing]; He is my God, and I will praise Him; my father's God, and I will exalt Him. The LORD is a man of war; the LORD is His name.

EXODUS 15:2–3

God is the Lord who heals you.

If you diligently heed the voice of the LORD your God and do what is right in His sight, give ear to His commandments and keep all His statutes, I will put none of the diseases on you which I have brought on the Egyptians. For I am the LORD who heals you.

EXODUS 15:26

Benny Hinn

IN THE GOSPEL OF JOHN, the Lord Jesus told Nicodemus, "And as Moses lifted up the serpent in the wilderness, even so must the Son of Man be lifted up" (John 3:14).

What was He talking about? God commanded Moses to construct a bronze serpent and place it on a pole. Why? . . . The Word of God says that whoever looked on that bronze serpent was healed. . . . Christ on the cross, bearing the sins of mankind upon His own body is powerfully pictured by this symbol.

Serpents had bitten the people in the wilderness, and many of them were dying. God told Moses that if the people would look upon the bronze serpent, they would live. . . . The word "looketh" implies faith. Those who look believe for a healing. Whoever believes that Jesus came and died, and is the Savior and the Healer, will be healed. Whoever looks up to the Lord Jesus on the cross with eyes of faith will find wholeness.

HEALING IN EVERY
BOOK OF THE BIBLE
⁓

The Miracle of Healing

God heals the body of every disease.

If the body develops a boil in the skin, and it is healed. . . .

LEVITICUS 13:18

God cleanses and purifies us from every evidence of sickness.

But if the scale appears to be at a standstill, and there is black hair grown up in it, the scale has healed. He is clean, and the priest shall pronounce him clean.

LEVITICUS 13:37

Declare the victory of your healing to the man of God and God's people.

The priest shall go out of the camp, and the priest shall examine him. . . . If the priest comes in and examines it, and indeed the plague has not spread in the house after the house was plastered, then the priest shall pronounce the house clean, because the plague is healed.

LEVITICUS 14:3, 48

Benny Hinn

MANY CHRISTIANS TODAY have the wrong picture of God.

From their childhood they have built an image of an almighty God who is harsh and austere—with glaring eyes of steel. They see Him with a whip in His hand, ready to beat them every time they make the slightest mistake.

But God is nothing like that. Though He occasionally chastises us for our good, He is always gentle, kind, and loving to His children.

I love what it says in the great hymn "Praise My Soul, the King of Heaven."

Father-like, He tends and spares us;
Well our feeble frame He knows,
In His hands He gently bears us,
Rescues us from all our foes.

THE BLOOD

Ask God for your healing.

Moses cried out to the LORD, saying, "Please heal her, O God, I pray!"

NUMBERS 12:13

God will deliver you out of your bondage and affliction.

I am the LORD your God, who brought you out of the land of Egypt, to be your God: I am the LORD your God.

NUMBERS 15:41

Let the healing waters of God's Spirit spring up in you.

Then Israel sang this song: "Spring up, O well! All of you sing to it."

NUMBERS 21:17

"Why doesn't God answer my prayer?"

*"Why can't I receive my deliverance
and my healing?"*

THE ANSWER TO your most
urgent need is close—much closer
than you ever imagined. Just
a word, spoken from your heart,
can cause life's darkest clouds
suddenly to disappear. It's time
to stop thinking that God is an
unapproachable spirit residing
millions of miles away. The Father
is so near that you can talk to
Him at any moment, and His
Spirit is so close that He can give
you comfort, peace, and direction.
All you have to do is ask and
trust that He will act.

What I have found in the Spirit is
not some mystery-shrouded secret.
It is as real as life itself and as close
as your very heartbeat.

GOOD MORNING
HOLY SPIRIT

The Miracle of Healing

Trust and obey God for your healing.

Now it shall come to pass, if you diligently obey the voice of the LORD your God, to observe carefully all His commandments which I command you today, that the LORD your God will set you high above all nations of the earth. And all these blessings shall come on you and overtake you, because you obey the voice of the LORD your God.

DEUTERONOMY 28:1–2

Move ahead with God for your healing.

And the LORD will make you the head and not the tail; you shall be above only, and not be beneath, if you heed the commandments of the LORD your God, which I command you today, and are careful to observe them.

DEUTERONOMY 28:13

God alone is the source of your healing.

Now see that I, even I, am He, and there is no God besides Me; I kill and I make alive; I wound and I heal; nor is there any who can deliver from My hand.

DEUTERONOMY 32:39

THERE ARE TWO realms of healing: there is the natural and the divine. The natural realm includes doctors, nutrition, exercise, and the things you and I have to do as human begins to keep healthy. You cannot expect to live a healthy life if you eat wrong and live wrong. We cannot ignore the natural. God gave us the natural realm. But I believe that faith begins when ability stops. God will not do for you what you can do for yourself. God expects you to use what you have in the natural. But when the natural comes to an end, then we enter into the divine and trust in the Lord. . . .

The divine realm requires faith. The Bible declares, *without faith it is impossible to please Him, for he who comes to God must believe that He is.* But please understand also that faith is a gift. When you need a healing, God supplies the faith for it. I want you to know that. And also remember that our God always comes on time. He doesn't always heal you when you want it. He heals you when He wants it. But while you are waiting for God to heal you, He'll give you the grace and the strength to wait.

THE NATURAL AND SPIRITUAL REALM OF HEALING

The Miracle of Healing

Possess your healing.

Every place that the sole of your foot will tread upon I have given you, as I said to Moses.

Joshua 1:3

While waiting for your healing, do not be discouraged. God is with you.

Have I not commanded you? Be strong and of good courage; be not afraid, nor be dismayed, for the LORD your God is with you wherever you go.

Joshua 1:9

Rest in your healing.

The LORD your God is giving you rest and is giving you this land.

Joshua 1:13b

Benny Hinn

Follow these seven keys for healing.

1. Trust God.
2. Keep His Word.
3. Confess your faults one to another.
4. Guard your tongue, speaking words of faith and not words of doubt and unbelief.
5. Stay in prayer, reminding God of His promises.
6. Resist the devil by submitting to God. When you do, the devil will flee from you.
7. Observe the laws of nature. Don't abuse your physical body through improper nutrition, lack of proper rest, and undue stress. . . .

ONCE YOU HAVE RECEIVED a miracle and been freed from the bondage of sickness and disease, you must treasure that miracle. Thank God for His touch and give Him the glory continually.

THE DAY
AFTER A MIRACLE

The Miracle of Healing

Judges Ruth

What God has covenanted for your healing, He will perform.

I will never break My covenant with you.

JUDGES 2:2b

Call upon God to restore your strength.

Then Samson called to the LORD saying, "O Lord GOD, remember me, I pray! Strengthen me, I pray, just this once. . . ."

JUDGES 16:28

Trust in God and come under His wings of healing, refuge, and protection.

The LORD repay your work, and a full reward be given you by the LORD God of Israel, under whose wings you have come for refuge.

RUTH 2:12

Benny Hinn

SAMSON WAS AT one time a man of great strength. Judges 16:29 presents the picture of a man who had been physically broken and taken captive by the Philistines. He was shackled and chained to the pillars. In addition, the Philistines had gouged out his eyes, drained his strength, humiliated and abused him, and threw him into prison as a slave. A captive of his enemies, the man was sick and blind. But in that seemingly hopeless setting, God gave him supernatural health and strength at the moment he prayed.

Supernatural strength poured into him, and in that moment Samson pushed over the giant pillars. . . . God touched him mightily as he called out to God in prayer, and in that one act, Samson destroyed more enemies than he had throughout his entire life. God supernaturally touched Samson's body, and in an instant his strength was miraculously restored with might and power.

HEALING IN EVERY
BOOK OF THE BIBLE

The Miracle of Healing

Repent and open the door to God's healing.

If you send away the ark of the God of Israel, do not send it empty; but by all means return it to Him with a trespass offering. Then you will be healed, and it will be known to you why His hand is not removed from you.

1 SAMUEL 6:3

God will fight your battles against illness and affliction.

All this assembly shall know that the LORD does not save with sword and spear; for the battle is the LORD's, and He will give you into our hands.

1 SAMUEL 17:47

The Lord is your Savior from the violence of illness.

The LORD is my rock and my fortress and my deliverer;
The God of my strength, in whom I will trust;
My shield and the horn of my salvation,
My stronghold and my refuge;
My Savior, You save me from violence.

2 SAMUEL 22:3

Benny Hinn

IN MARK 12:30 we read, "And you shall love the LORD your God with all your heart, and with all your soul, with all your mind, and with all your strength."

To love God with all your heart means with every atom of your being. He wants you to love Him supremely and with everything that is within you.

When you are commanded to love God with all your soul, you are to love Him with all your emotions and your intellectual will. He wants everything in your emotions and intellect to love Him.

When you love God with all your mind, you love Him with everything you understand about Him. . . .

When you love Him with all your strength, you love God with everything about you physically as well as in your service to Him and in your daily walk.

THE BIBLICAL
ROAD TO BLESSING

The Miracle of Healing

Accept and receive God's provision for the journey of your healing.

And the angel of the LORD came back the second time, and touched him, and said, "Arise and eat, because the journey is too great for you."

1 KINGS 19:7

God heals the dead and barren places of your life with living waters.

Thus says the LORD: "I have healed this water; from it there shall be no more death or barrenness."

2 KINGS 2:21

Go up into God's house and be healed.

Return and tell Hezekiah the leader of My people, "Thus says the LORD, the God of David your father: 'I have heard your prayer, I have seen your tears; surely, I will heal you. On the third day you shall go up to the house of the LORD'".

2 KINGS 20:5

Benny Hinn

THE SPIRIT OF GOD is the
planet's lifeline for survival.

Without Him we'd be like a
deep-sea diver whose oxygen was
suddenly cut off. The Holy Spirit
has been given an awesome task:
to *create, maintain, and renew*—
in both our physical body and
the material world. . . .

Why am I breathing? Why am
I alive? The Scripture declares
that it is because the Spirit of God
has placed breath in my nostrils
(Job 27:3). He's enabling me to live.
Not only spiritually, but He is the
source of my physical being. God's
Word declares that the same Spirit
that raised the Lord Jesus from the
dead dwells in you as a believer and
He will quicken your mortal body.

Life without the Holy Spirit is
really no life at all.

WELCOME,
HOLY SPIRIT

The Miracle of Healing

Seek God's strength in your weakness.

Seek the LORD and His strength;
Seek His face evermore!

1 CHRONICLES 16:11

Pray for healing in the land.

If My people, who are called by My name will humble
themselves, and pray and seek My face, and turn from
their wicked ways, then I will hear from heaven, and
will forgive their sin and heal their land.

2 CHRONICLES 7:14

Ask your leaders to pray for your healing.

And the LORD listened to Hezekiah and healed
the people.

2 CHRONICLES 30:20

Benny Hinn

GOD'S LOVE FOR His children and His willingness to bless are clearly illustrated in His dealings with the children of Israel. His faithfulness to them year after year extended into every aspect of their lives. And the promises of God to the children of Israel found throughout the old covenant extend to you and me as His children today.

When we experience no lack, God is meeting our *need*, not our *greed*. Notice that the Israelites weren't provided new shoes; rather, the heavenly Father superintended over them such that the shoes they had never wore out. . . .

Our loving heavenly Father promises to make the nation of Israel a testimony of His faithfulness to bless generation after generation.

THE BIBLICAL
ROAD TO BLESSING

The Miracle of Healing

When God empowers your body with strength, His healing power is at work.

And they kept the Feast of Unleavened Bread seven days with joy; for the LORD made them joyful, and turned the heart of the king of Assyria toward them, to strengthen their hands in the work of the house of God, the God of Israel.

Ezra 6:22

Let God's joy be your strength.

Do not sorrow, for the joy of the LORD is your strength.

Nehemiah 8:10

Benny Hinn

GOD ALMIGHTY wants you
well and healthy.

Divine health is and always has
been better than divine healing.
Divine health was always God's
plan for man. When we examine
Adam's life in the Garden of Eden
before the fall, we find that he was
healthy and had dominion over
everything. Sickness entered the
human race after Adam's sin. God
created Adam healthy—a perfect
act of creation. We find no record
of sickness until after sin entered
the world. . . .

The Word of the Lord declares
that God sent His son, and because
Jesus came, no sickness has any
legal right over you. I believe
that it is possible for each of us
to grasp this truth and to realize
the reality of our inheritance of
healing and health.

THE DAY AFTER
A MIRACLE

The Miracle of Healing

As a child of the King you can come into God's presence at any time.

Esther put on her royal robes and stood in the inner court of the king's palace, across from the king's house, while the king sat on his royal throne in the royal house, facing the entrance of the house.

ESTHER 5:1

God will restore the light to your life.

He will redeem his soul from going down to the Pit, and his life shall see the light.

JOB 33:28

GOD WANTS TO bless His children. As a father, I love to give gifts to my children and provide for them. And nothing brings me greater joy than to see the twinkle in their eyes as they unwrap a gift or to hear them giggle with delight as I give them something they have desired.

If a mere human being like me can find such joy through giving gifts to my children, just imagine how much joy our heavenly Father receives when He bestows good gifts upon us. Truly, our loving heavenly Father longs to bless His children—if for no other reason than for the pure joy of knowing the pleasure *we* receive when He provides for us.

How easy it can be to miss this very simple principle: God loves you and wants the very best for you. *He really does.*

THE BIBLICAL ROAD
TO BLESSING

The Miracle of Healing

Sing, pray, and declare these truths from the Psalms:

Have mercy on me, O LORD, for I am weak;
O LORD, heal me, for my bones are troubled.

PSALM 6:2

O LORD my God, I cried out to You,
And You healed me.

PSALM 30:2

I said, "LORD, be merciful to me;
Heal my soul, for I have sinned against You."

PSALM 41:4

I RECENTLY TALKED to a man who experienced a glorious healing from colon cancer more than two years ago. We were discussing how marvelous it is to be touched by God's miracle-working power, and to step from death into life as health is restored by God's grace. As I listened to him talk about his miracle and the time since, I heard him say something very important. He said that he never fails to thank God each day for his healing and to testify to others about God's healing touch. He never takes his miracle or his health for granted. He thanks God for health and healing for today and every day.

If you have received a miracle, remember to give God the glory. This is an important weapon against the enemy. A miracle is not received because of self worth; it is given because of God's grace. Never fail to give Him thanks.

THE DAY AFTER
A MIRACLE

The Miracle of Healing

Why are you cast down, O my soul?
And why are you disquieted within me?
Hope in God;
For I shall yet praise Him,
The help of my countenance and my God.

PSALM 42:11

O LORD, open my lips,
And my mouth shall show forth Your praise.

PSALM 51:15

You have made the earth tremble;
You have broken it;
Heal its breaches, for it is shaking.

PSALM 60:2

Benny Hinn

As the Holy Spirit begins
to work in the depths of your soul,
He strengthens you spiritually
with spiritual strength and maturity
that gives you an even greater level
of faith and enables you to trust
God for the *impossible* and believe
Him for the *invisible*. No matter
what the obstacle, no matter
what challenge you may face, you
will say with the Psalmist: "The
Lord is my light and my salvation;
whom shall I fear? The Lord is
the strength of my life; of whom
shall I be afraid?" (Ps. 27:1).
That strength comes from deep
within as the Holy Spirit brings
fearless, and sometimes even
violent faith to your life.

That Your way may be known on earth,
Your salvation among all nations.

PSALM 67:2

Who forgives all your iniquities;
Who heals all your diseases.

PSALM 103:3

He sent His word and healed them,
And delivered them from their destructions.

PSALM 107:20

He heals the brokenhearted
And binds up their wounds.

PSALM 147:3

Benny Hinn

GOD SENT His Son to die on the
cross to guarantee your salvation
and to make a way for your healing.

This is the source of all hope.
You can get up and go on because
Christ has given eternal life to
every person who believes in Him.
No sickness, heartache, pain, or
even death can take that away.

Always remember, Jesus
knows every pain you feel. He
hears your cries and His heart
is full of mercy for you. In His
sovereign grace, that moment
will come when He will say,
"This is your day for a miracle!"

Bless the LORD O my soul:
And all that is within me,
bless His holy name!
Psalm 103:1

THIS IS YOUR DAY
FOR A MIRACLE

The Miracle of Healing

Fear the Lord and . . .

It will be health to your flesh,
And strength to your bones.

PROVERBS 3:8

God's Word to you is healing and life.

My son, give attention to my words; . . .
For they are life to those who find them,
And health to all their flesh.

PROVERBS 4:22

Speak pleasant words of healing.

Pleasant words are like a honeycomb,
Sweetness to the soul and health to the bones.

PROVERBS 16:24

Benny Hinn

IT IS SO natural to be ungrateful, and it's just as natural to be thankful only for the things that seem good at the time. But when the Holy Spirit has control, you will be able to give thanks all the time, and for everything that comes your way—even the things that are not pleasant. The Word says, "In everything give thanks; for this is the will of God in Christ Jesus for you" (1 Thess. 5:18).

When you are walking with the Holy Spirit, He is constantly prompting you to say, "Thank you, Lord." . . .

We are to give thanks at all times and in all things. . . .

We are instructed to recognize the Father and the Son as the source of all good things. But we thank them through the Holy Spirit.

If you haven't experienced the healing that comes from this thankfulness, don't wait another moment. Let the Holy Spirit bring healing to your perspective!

WELCOME,
HOLY SPIRIT

The Miracle of Healing

The time for your healing has been established by the God who heals.

A time to kill,
And a time to heal;
A time to break down,
And a time to build up.

ECCLESIASTES 3:3

Come to God's banquet table and sit under His healing banner of love.

He brought me to the banqueting house,
And his banner over me was love.

SONG OF SOLOMON 2:4

Ask God to remove every spot in you.

You are all fair, my love,
And there is no spot in you.

SONG OF SOLOMON 4:7

Benny Hinn

As a FATHER, I cannot even begin to fathom the pain that our wonderful heavenly Father endured by allowing His Son to die the terrible death of Calvary.

I do everything in my power to prevent anything bad from happening to my children. I'm concerned when they have a bad day at school or when they scrape a knee while playing. Oh, how the Father's heart must have ached as He watched His precious, perfect Son—rejected by the people He came to save—spat upon, scourged, sliced with a crown of thorns, and crucified among criminals and curs!

Oh, my friend, never doubt for even one moment the precious love of our wonderful heavenly Father for you and me. Truly, there is no other single greater thing that the Father could do to demonstrate His love for us than send His Son to die in our place and for our sins.

The Miracle of Healing

God heals every wound.

*Moreover the light of the moon will be as the light
    of the sun,
And the light of the sun will be sevenfold,
As the light of seven days,
In the day that the LORD binds up the bruise of
    His people
And heals the stroke of their wound.*

ISAIAH 30:26

By Christ's stripes, you are healed.

*Surely He has borne our griefs
And carried our sorrows;
Yet we esteemed Him stricken,
Smitten by God, and afflicted.
But He was wounded for our transgressions,
He was bruised for our iniquities;
The chastisement of our peace was upon Him;
And by His stripes we are healed.*

ISAIAH 53:4–5

Benny Hinn

ON THE CROSS Jesus bore our sins
and the consequences of our sins.

Surely He has borne our griefs
And carried our sorrows (Is. 53:4).

The word *grief* here is the
Hebrew *choliy,* which means
"weak, sick, or afflicted." Surely
He has borne our weaknesses,
sicknesses, and afflictions. The
Hebrew word for *sorrows* is *makob,*
which means "pain or grief."

The Scriptures are clear: Jesus not
only died to take away our sins; He
died to take away our sicknesses.

THE BLOOD

The Miracle of Healing

God sees your need and will heal you.

"I have seen his ways, and will heal him;
I will also lead him,
And restore comforts to him
And to his mourners.
I create the fruit of the lips:
Peace, peace to him who is far off and to him
    who is near,"
Says the LORD, "And I will heal him."

ISAIAH 57:18–19

Your healing is speeding your way.

Then your light shall break forth like the morning,
Your healing shall spring forth speedily,
And your righteousness shall go before you;
The glory of the LORD shall be your rear guard.

ISAIAH 58:8

Benny Hinn

I REMEMBER a lady who went
to Katherine Kuhlman's meetings
eleven times before she was healed.
Eleven times!

I asked one day, "Why did you
keep going back?"

She said, "Because I knew.
I knew my day was coming, and
I was going to go back until God
healed me. I was not giving up."

The reason many do not get
healed is because they give up so
quickly. Remember, faith is vital
and the prayer of faith is important.
You see, faith not only prays, faith
acts. Let me say quickly, that when
God heals, He imparts the faith
necessary for the healing. . . .
He gives us a measure of faith. . . .
God imparts faith to those who
need a healing through His Spirit.
So you don't have to struggle
or beg—just receive!

The Bible says, *"The prayer of faith
will save the sick."*

THE SPIRITUAL AND NATURAL
REALM OF HEALING

The Miracle of Healing

Return to God and He will heal your backsliding.

Return, you backsliding children,
And I will heal your backslidings.
Indeed we do come to You,
For You are the Lord our God.

Jeremiah 3:22

There is a balm in Gilead—Jesus!

Is there no balm in Gilead,
Is there no physician there?
Why then is there no recovery
For the health of the daughter of my people?

Jeremiah 8:22

Ask God to heal you.

Heal me, O Lord, and I shall be healed;
Save me, and I shall be saved,
For you are my praise.

Jeremiah 17:14

Benny Hinn

WHEN WE PUT our trust (faith) in God, we will reap a good harvest, one that is faith-filled and prosperous. . . .

Jeremiah 17 verse 7 says, "Blessed is the man who trusts in the LORD, and whose hope is the LORD. For he shall be like a tree planted by the waters, which spreads out its roots by the river, and will not fear when heat comes, but its leaf will be green. . . ."

In the natural, as a tree matures the root structure increases. This helps to support the added height and growth of the tree, and to bring the water and nourishment the tree needs to survive and continue growing. Spiritually, we must be like the tree. Our roots or our faith must go deeper to bring stability and promote spiritual growth. The water of the Word brings life, and we receive nourishment. As we understand and apply the Word of God to our lives, we are able to appropriate God's promises for our life and receive what is ours as a believer.

THE DAY AFTER
A MIRACLE

The Miracle of Healing

God will restore your health.

"For I will restore health to you
And heal you of your wounds," says the LORD,
"Because they called you an outcast, saying:
'This is Zion; no one seeks her.'"

JEREMIAH 30:17

God is your source of health and healing.

Behold, I will bring it health and healing; I will
heal them and reveal to them the abundance of
peace and truth.

JEREMIAH 33:6

Seek God's mercy for your healing.

Through the LORD'S *mercies we are not consumed,*
Because His compassions fail not.
They are new every morning;
Great is Your faithfulness.

LAMENTATIONS 3:22–23

DOCTORS AND MEDICAL science
have helped many individuals
and continue to help many as
their commitment to medical
research unlocks the secrets of
life-threatening diseases. But when
you have exhausted every possible
resource and there is nowhere else
to go for help in the natural, there
is still an answer—go to Jesus.

Even today many choose
not to come to Jesus because they
are afraid of losing something—
friends, a job, respect, or some
status in society. They face the same
forms of opposition that Jairus did
[in Mark 5:23–24].

When Jairus came to Jesus,
he had only one thing on his mind—
he wanted his daughter to live.

His desire for his daughter
to live surpassed any fear of
loss that could oppose him.
He overcame the fear of loss and
moved closer to his miracle.

DON'T GIVE UP!

The Miracle of Healing

Seek the healing of your heart.

I give you a new heart and put a new spirit within you; I will take the heart of stone out of your flesh and give you a heart of flesh.

EZEKIEL 36:26

Come to God's living waters and be healed.

This water flows toward the eastern region, goes down into the valley, and enters the sea. When it reaches the sea, its waters are healed.

EZEKIEL 47:8

Drink in your healing from the river of God.

And it shall be that every living thing that moves, wherever the rivers go, will live. There will be a very great multitude of fish, because these waters go there; for they will be healed, and everything will live wherever the river goes.

EZEKIEL 47:9

Benny Hinn

SEATED WITH MY son, Joshua, on my lap, I relaxed for a few moments, musing over the activities of the day. . . . I glanced down at Joshua and noticed that he was fast asleep in my arms. He looked so peaceful lying there. . . .

In that tender moment, as I held my sleeping child in my arms, the love that I felt as a father was so rich. But as the Lord spoke to my heart, comparing the love I felt toward Joshua with the greatness of His tender love for me, I understood how weak and frail my love for my son was when compared to God the Father's infinite love for us His children.

As a father, there is nothing that I would not do for my [children]. . . . But my love for them, along with my ability and willingness to lovingly provide and care for them, cannot begin to compare with the wonderful, loyal love that our heavenly Father has for you and me—a love that has never been more in evidence than it was on Calvary.

THE BIBLICAL ROAD
TO BLESSING

The Miracle of Healing

Come to the Ancient of Days for your healing.

I watched till thrones were put in place,
And the Ancient of Days was seated;
His garment was white as snow,
And the hair of his head was like pure wool.

DANIEL 7:9

Know God your Healer and be strong in Him.

Those who do wickedly against the covenant he shall
corrupt with flattery; but the people who know their
God shall be strong, and carry out great exploits.

DANIEL 11:32B

Be wise and turn others to God your Healer.

Those who are wise shall shine
Like the brightness of the firmament,
And those who turn many to righteousness
Like the stars forever and ever.

DANIEL 12:3

Benny Hinn

IF HEALING was extended to one person, as it was in so many instances throughout the Bible, then it is available to all. Miracles are not selectively bestowed upon those deemed worthy but are available to every man, woman, boy, and girl. That includes YOU!

God's healing power is not limited to a time frame in history or to certain individuals. He is the "God of miracles," a gracious, loving, unchanging Father who has and always will work the impossible in the lives of mortal men when we reach out to Him and ask in faith, expecting to receive.

God's promise for healing and health is the same to this generation that it has been to every generation throughout history.

DON'T GIVE UP!

The Miracle of Healing

Turn to God and be healed.

Come, and let us return unto the LORD;
For He has torn, but He will heal us;
He has stricken, but He will bind us up.

HOSEA 6:1

Let God take you into His arms and heal you.

I taught Ephraim to walk,
Taking them by their arms;
But they did not know that I healed them.

HOSEA 11:3

Repent and be healed of your backsliding.

I will heal their backsliding,
I will love them freely,
For My anger has turned away from him.

HOSEA 14:4

Benny Hinn

WHEN MY OLDEST daughter Jessica was just a toddler, I remember taking her for a walk in the woods. As we were about to walk up a little hill, I reached down and took hold of her hand. I didn't want her to slip and fall.

Jessica's little hand was too weak to hold on to mine. She was depending on my strength to help her reach the top of the hill.

Then the Holy Spirit said to me, "Who is holding your hand?"

As I thought about it, I said, "You are, Lord."

How true it is. All of us are like my little girl Jessica. We're too weak to hold on to His hand. He holds on to our hands.

The Bible says, "For I, the Lord your God, will hold your right hand, saying to you, 'Fear not, I will help you'" (Is. 41:13).

THE BLOOD

The Miracle of Healing

Let God pour out His healing Spirit upon you.

And it shall come to pass afterward
That I will pour out My spirit on all flesh;
Your sons and your daughters shall prophesy,
Your old men shall dream dreams,
Your young men shall see visions.

JOEL 2:28

Are you sick and weak? Say you are strong in the Lord your God.

Beat your plowshares into swords
And your pruning hooks into spears;
Let the weak say, "I am strong."

JOEL 3:10

Seek good, and God the Healer will be with you.

Seek good and not evil,
That you may live;
So the LORD God of hosts will be with you,
As you have spoken.

AMOS 5:14

Benny Hinn

GOD HAS WILLED that all His children live in divine health. *I wish above all things that you prosper and be in health as your soul prospers*, the Bible says. God's divine desire is for His people to prosper and be in health. That's the word of God, but sadly today so many are sick, and it's not supposed to be that way.

I know we live in a society with a lot of poison in the air and poison in our food, but I believe what the Bible says. *He'll bless your bread and bless your water if you will obey Him.* You see, what you cannot do, God will do. I'll never forget the Lord saying to me one day, "I'll protect you when you don't know. But when you *know*, you're responsible." So there are times when we don't know what's in our food, but that's when God protects us.

HEALING IN EVERY
BOOK OF THE BIBLE

The Miracle of Healing

Look to God upon Mt. Zion for deliverance from your illness.

But on Mount Zion there shall be deliverance,
And there shall be holiness;
The house of Jacob shall possess their possessions.

OBADIAH 17

Begin to thank God for your healing and give Him what you have vowed.

But I will sacrifice to You
With the voice of thanksgiving;
I will pay what I have vowed.
Salvation is of the LORD.

JONAH 2:9

Follow your healing with obedience.

He has shown you, O man, what is good;
And what does the LORD require of you
But to do justly,
To love mercy,
And to walk humbly with your God?

MICAH 6:8

Benny Hinn

MY MOTHER ALWAYS put so much love into her cooking, and the fragrance of whatever she was preparing filled our house. . . . With several growing boys in the family, leftovers were never a problem. I don't like leftovers—and neither does the Lord, for He is always asking us for our best, not our leftovers.

So before we can really appreciate the Bible's principles on how God wants us to handle the resources He has blessed us with, we must first do one important thing: surrender everything to Him.

Now surrender isn't just talk. . . . Surrender is prayerfully saying, "Lord, You own my body, You own the work of my hands, You own my family, You own my possessions. Everything I have is Yours. You are Lord, indeed. And I want You to own my heart too." That's surrender.

THE BIBLICAL ROAD
TO BLESSING

The Miracle of Healing

Declare the good news about your Healer.

Behold, on the mountains
The feet of him who brings good tidings,
Who proclaims peace!

NAHUM 1:15A

Fill the earth with the knowledge that God heals.

For the earth will be filled
With the knowledge of the glory of the LORD,
As the waters cover the sea.

HABAKKUK 2:14

God's healing fills you with joy, rest, and love.

The LORD, your God in your midst,
The Mighty One, will save,
He will rejoice over you with gladness,
He will quiet you with His love,
He will rejoice over you with singing.

ZEPHANIAH 3:17

Benny Hinn

AFTER YOU HAVE received your
miracle, turn away from those who
oppose miracles. . . .

Stay away from individuals
who will speak faith-destroying
words—idle words—which bring
doubt, unbelief, and death.
Surround yourself with faith-filled
believers who will agree with you,
strengthen you, build your faith,
and rejoice with you because of
your miracle.

Continue to see yourself well
and whole, healed in Jesus' name.
Experience the rich inheritance
that is yours through Jesus Christ!
Learn what God's Word promises,
and stand on those promises.
Say goodbye to doubt and unbelief.
Trust the God who healed you to
keep you today and every day.

THE DAY AFTER
A MIRACLE

The Miracle of Healing

Do not be afraid.

According to the word that I covenanted with you when you came out of Egypt, so My Spirit remains among you; do not fear!

HAGGAI 2:5

You will not be healed by your might or power—only by God's Spirit.

"Not by might nor by power, but by My Spirit," says the LORD of hosts.

ZECHARIAH 4:6

Jesus Christ goes before you with healing in His wings.

*But to you who fear My name
The Sun of Righteousness shall arise
With healing in His wings;
And you shall go out
And grow fat like stall-fed calves.*

MALACHI 4:2

Benny Hinn

THE BIBLE IS filled with glorious accounts of miracles. Throughout the ministry of Jesus, Scripture reveals many occasions when He supernaturally intervened in the lives of men and women. From turning water into wine at Canaan to raising Jairus' daughter from the dead, he brought help and hope to desperate lives. . . . There was no disease or condition that was too difficult for Jesus to heal. He had power over all diseases. . . .

The same Jesus who walked this earth "healing all manner of sickness and all manner of disease among the people" still heals today. Diseases and infirmities still vanish as sick bodies are transformed by the healing touch of Jesus. Health and life are restored when the master comes on the scene.

DON'T GIVE UP!

The Miracle of Healing

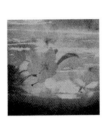

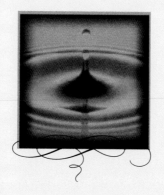

Promises of Healing
from the NEW TESTAMENT

Jesus heals all kinds of disease.

And Jesus went about all Galilee, teaching in their synagogues, preaching the gospel of the kingdom, and healing all kinds of sickness and all kinds of disease among the people.

MATTHEW 4:23

Your faith has made you well.

But Jesus turned around, and when He saw her He said, "Be of good cheer, daughter; your faith has made you well." And the woman was made well from that hour.

MATTHEW 9:22

Your illness moves Jesus with compassion.

And when Jesus went out He saw a great multitude; and He was moved with compassion for them, and healed their sick.

MATTHEW 14:14

Benny Hinn

Do you remember the woman who tried to touch the hem of Jesus garment? It was not the touch of her hand that brought healing— it was the touch of her faith. When the woman touched the hem of the Lord's garment, He felt virtue go out of Him and said, "Who touched me?"

And Peter said, "Lord, many are touching you." But Jesus said, "No, someone *touched* me." There were many hands touching Him in the natural, but only one woman touched Him in faith.

You say, "How do we touch Him?" You touch Him with your trust, when you depend on Him. It's so simple. So simple.

THE NATURAL AND SPIRITUAL
REALM OF HEALING

The Miracle of Healing

Reach out to Jesus and be healed.

For He healed many, so that as many as had afflictions pressed about Him to touch Him.

MARK 3:10

Jesus can cast out all demons.

And they cast out many demons, and anointed with oil many who were sick, and healed them.

MARK 6:13

Touch Jesus and be made well.

Wherever He entered, into villages, cities, or the country, they laid the sick in the marketplaces, and begged Him that they might just touch the hem of His garment. And as many as touched Him were made well.

MARK 6:56

Benny Hinn

WHILE IT IS true that God
is sovereign and can do what
He wishes, it is also true that
God delights when we show our
love by trusting Him enough to
do what He says. And I don't mean
by this simply mental agreement
with God—I mean a faith
that manifests itself in action.
That's real faith, and God's loving
response to this is to put His
mighty resurrection power
at our disposal. . . .

Often in our crusades, I'll tell
people to touch the part of their
body that they want God to heal.
I'll encourage them to begin
moving their afflicted arms or
bending their hurting legs. These
actions do nothing in themselves,
but they *do* demonstrate that the
person has faith in God's healing
power. And in the Scriptures you
see again and again that when the
Lord Jesus healed the sick He
asked them to *do* something
before the miracle took place.

WELCOME,
HOLY SPIRIT
~

The Miracle of Healing

Jesus heals the brokenhearted.

The Spirit of the LORD is upon me,
Because He has anointed Me
To preach the gospel to the poor;
He has sent Me to heal the brokenhearted,
To proclaim liberty to the captives
And recovery of sight to the blind,
To set at liberty those who are oppressed.

LUKE 4:18

Jesus is coming to lay hands on you for your healing.

When the sun was setting, all those who had any that
were sick with various diseases brought them to Him;
and He laid His hands on every one of them and
healed them.

LUKE 4:40

Benny Hinn

I HAVE OFTEN wondered why, in my own meetings, the Spirit directs me so often to pray for healing. And I have wondered why my ministry has been accompanied by people who fall under the power of the Holy Spirit. But when I look at the results of the meetings, I see that every manifestation of the Spirit is for one purpose: to bring people to Christ.

It is a demonstration that God is alive, that He is still "moving" in the lives of people. I have seen thousands of people literally fall under the power of the Spirit, and I believe that just a small touch of God's power is all they felt. But it demonstrates the awesome strength of the Almighty, and it draws people to the Savior.

Being healed or even being "slain in the Spirit" is not a prerequisite for heaven. There is only one door—Christ the Lord.

GOOD MORNING,
HOLY SPIRIT

The Miracle of Healing

The power of the Lord is present to heal you.

Now it happened that on a certain day, as He was teaching, that there were Pharisees and teachers of the law sitting by, who had come out of every town of Galilee, and Judea, and Jerusalem. And the power of the Lord was present to heal them.

LUKE 5:17

PICTURE, if you will, God the Father sitting on His throne in heaven and Jesus on earth healing the sick and performing miracles. And what about the Holy Spirit? He's the channel, the contact between both personalities. . . .

Picture this. Jesus is walking past a man who is very sick. The Father picks up the phone (as if He needed one) and says, "Holy Spirit? Stop Jesus! Tell Him to halt right where He is."

The Spirit says, "Okay. Jesus, stop."

He speaks into the phone and says, "Father, what should He do?"

"Tell Him to heal that man," says the voice of God.

Jesus immediately lays His hands on the man, the power of the Spirit flowing through Him, and the man is miraculously raised up.

GOOD MORNING,
HOLY SPIRIT

The Miracle of Healing

Are you at the point of death? Only Jesus can heal you.

When he heard that Jesus had come out of Judea into Galilee, he went to Him and implored Him to come down and heal his son, for he was at the point of death.

JOHN 4:47

Ask yourself, do you really want to be made well?

When Jesus saw him lying there, and knew that he had already been in that condition a long time, He said to him, "Do you want to be made well?"

JOHN 5:6

Be healed and sin no more.

Afterward Jesus found him in the temple, and said to him, "See, you have been made well. Sin no more, lest a worse thing come upon you."

JOHN 5:14

Why Jesus still heals today:

1. **Jesus heals because He has compassion.**
   Because of what He endured on the cross,
   the Lord fully understands the pain and
   suffering we experience.

2. **Jesus heals to bring glory to His father.**
   Christ knew the source of His power and
   continually reminded people that He had
   come to do the work of His father.

3. **Jesus heals to fulfill the Father's promise.**
   The miracles of Christ . . . are the fulfillment
   of God's promises spoken through His
   prophets to us His people.

4. **Healing belongs to His children.**
   God heals without respect of persons.

5. **Healing demonstrates the power of God.**

6. **Healing demonstrates the power of His blood.**
   Christ's death on the cross was not only for
   your salvation, but for your healing.

7. **Jesus heals to destroy the works of the devil.**
   Every time someone is healed, Satan is dealt
   a devastating blow.

THIS IS YOUR DAY
FOR A MIRACLE

The Miracle of Healing

Ask the Lord to stretch forth His hand to heal you.

Now, Lord, . . . grant to Your servants that with all boldness they may speak Your word, by stretching out Your hand to heal, and that signs and wonders may be done through the name of Your holy Servant Jesus.

ACTS 4:29–30

God desires that everyone be healed.

A multitude gathered from the surrounding cities to Jerusalem, bringing sick people and those who were tormented by unclean spirits, and they were all healed.

ACTS 5:16

Jesus is anointed to heal you.

God anointed Jesus of Nazareth with the Holy Spirit and with power, who went about doing good and healing all who were oppressed by the devil, for God was with Him.

ACTS 10:38

Benny Hinn

As PAUL and Barnabas ministered
from city to city, there was a power
in their preaching, an authority
and confirmation to their words
and deeds.

When they came to Lystra,
a man crippled from birth, who
had never walked, heard them.
And as Paul spoke, the man's faith
came alive, and Paul, perceiving
"that he had faith to be healed,"
said with a loud voice, "Stand
upright on your feet." And the
crippled man leaped to his feet
and began to walk.

Paul was watching the man
while he preached but waited
to speak until the man was ready
for his miracle. The Holy Spirit
gave Paul the perception to know
when the time for that miracle
was right.

WELCOME,
HOLY SPIRIT

The Miracle of Healing

Be dead to sin and sickness and alive in Christ.

Likewise you also, reckon yourselves to be dead indeed to sin, but alive to God in Christ Jesus our Lord.

ROMANS 6:11

Let the Spirit help you pray for your healing.

Likewise the Spirit also helps in our weaknesses. For we do not know what we should pray for as we ought, but the Spirit Himself makes intercession for us with groanings which cannot be uttered.

ROMANS 8:26

Trust that God is working for good in the midst of every situation in your life.

We know that all things work together for good to those who love God, to those who are the called according to His purpose.

ROMANS 8:28

Benny Hinn

FAITH IS VITAL to your miracle.
Healing is received by faith,
and healing is kept by faith.
Faith does not deny fact; it changes
it. Faith is not something that
comes by prayer. Rather, God's
Word states that "Faith comes by
hearing, and hearing by the Word"
(Romans 10:17). The word *hearing*
is in the present tense, suggesting
that we must continually "hear."

The word you heard yesterday
is not sufficient to sustain your
spiritual life indefinitely. Therefore,
we must allow God's Word to
continually wash over our spirit
so that faith can grow. Faith comes
by hearing and hearing and hearing
and hearing His Word. The truth
contained therein is what brings life
and sets us free and keeps us free.

THE DAY AFTER
A MIRACLE

The Miracle of Healing

Your body is the Temple of God's Spirit.

Do you not know that you are the temple of God and that the Spirit of God dwells in you?

1 CORINTHIANS 3:16

Seek out those with the gifts of healing in the church to pray for you.

The manifestation of the Spirit is given to each one for the profit of all: for to one is given the word of wisdom through the Spirit, . . . to another faith by the same Spirit, to another gifts of healings by the same Spirit.

1 CORINTHIANS 12:7–9

Claim in Christ the promise of God's healing.

For all the promises of God in Him are Yes, and in Him Amen, to the glory of God through us.

2 CORINTHIANS 1:20

Benny Hinn

ALWAYS REMEMBER that it's not ability but our *availability* that matters to God. When we make ourselves available to Him for service, we become a channel that He can anoint to bring His healing power and presence to the lives of others.

The same thing takes place in the miracle crusades. Those glorious miracles don't happen because of any ability I possess. I couldn't even heal an ant! Before I ever take one step onto the platform, I always invite the Holy Spirit to walk out with me. As I make myself available to God, He anoints me for Service. And as His power and presence flow through me in that service, it's not anything I possess that touches the people; it's the Lord. Much like a garden hose carries water to thirsty, wilting plants growing in parched soil, I'm just the channel He anoints and uses to bring God's healing power and presence to the hurting and spiritually hungry. I make myself available, and He does the rest!

WELCOME,
HOLY SPIRIT

The Miracle of Healing

Every curse, including sickness, has been broken by Christ.

Christ has redeemed us from the curse of the law, having become a curse for us (for it is written, "Cursed is everyone who hangs on a tree").

GALATIANS 3:13

Put on Christ and put on His healing.

For as many of you as were baptized into Christ have put on Christ.

GALATIANS 3:27

Wait and hope for your healing in Christ.

For we through the Spirit eagerly wait for the hope of righteousness by faith.

GALATIANS 5:5

Benny Hinn

WE KNOW THAT Jesus performed many miracles, yet He said of those who believe in Him: "Greater than these shall ye do" (John 14:12 KJV).

I wish I could explain signs, wonders, and healings, but I can't. All I know is that they did not cease with the ministry of Christ and the apostles. How can I be sure? At the very least from my own personal experience. I was born with a severe stuttering problem that completely disappeared the moment I stood up to preach my first sermon.

God confirms His Word and bears witness "with signs and wonders, with various miracles, and gifts of the Holy Spirit" (Heb. 2:4). Not just back then, but right now.

WELCOME,
HOLY SPIRIT

The Miracle of Healing

In Christ's blood, there is healing power.

*In Him we have redemption through His blood, the
forgiveness of sins, according to the riches of His grace.*

EPHESIANS 1:7

**God will do more in your healing than you can
ever imagine.**

*Now to Him who is able to do exceedingly
abundantly above all that we ask or think,
according to the power that works in us,
to Him be glory.*

EPHESIANS 3:20–21

**Put off the old sick man, and put on the new
man in Christ.**

*Put on the new man which was created according
to God, in true righteousness and holiness.*

EPHESIANS 4:24

Benny Hinn

WHENEVER YOU celebrate the
Lord's supper, remember that it is
because of the blood of Jesus Christ
that we can have fellowship with
God. And as we recall what He has
done for us when His body was
broken and His blood was shed,
then the presence of
God will descend.

I've seen in my own experience
that through the blood of Jesus,
the anointing of God always
comes—not only on my private,
personal prayer life, but even
during church services and the
great miracle services.

I never conduct a service
without thanking Him for the
blood. And every time I do, the
presence of God descends, and
miracles take place. In the old
covenant, God responded with fire
when blood was offered on the
altar. So it is today. When the
blood of Jesus is honored, when the
cross is honored, the Holy Spirit
comes and touches people's lives.

THE BLOOD

The Miracle of Healing

The good work of your healing will be completed.

Being confident of this very thing, that He who has begun a good work in you will complete it until the day of Jesus Christ.

<small>PHILIPPIANS 1:6</small>

Pray for your healing and do not worry.

Be anxious for nothing, but in everything by prayer and supplication, with thanksgiving, let your requests be made known to God.

<small>PHILIPPIANS 4:6</small>

Your need for healing will be supplied.

My God shall supply all your need according to His riches in glory by Christ Jesus.

<small>PHILIPPIANS 4:19</small>

REMEMBER, nothing is impossible when you put your trust in God!

The Bible states that if we have "faith as a grain of mustard seed," that's enough for God to work with. The Lord will intervene on your behalf. . . . A mustard seed is no larger than the head of a pin; yet, God's Word says that's big enough.

I heard that someone once said to Kathryn Kuhlman, "You must have great faith, Kathryn." She replied, "No, I have little faith in a great God." We can be confident in this fact—when our faith is small, our God is big!

Remember, Jesus is concerned about your faith. He will protect it until you get your miracle. Don't give up! Just believe!

DON'T GIVE UP!

The Miracle of Healing

Walk in Christ your healer.

As you therefore have received Christ Jesus the Lord, so walk in Him.

COLOSSIANS 2:6

Hide yourself in Christ and His healing.

You died, and your life is hidden with Christ in God.

COLOSSIANS 3:3

There is healing in God's Word.

Let the word of Christ dwell in you richly in all wisdom, teaching and admonishing one another in psalms and hymns and spiritual songs, singing with grace in your hearts to the Lord.

COLOSSIANS 3:16

Benny Hinn

I BELIEVE THAT faith is more than hope or expectation. Faith is alive because of a person. His name is Jesus. It is really quite simple. Where Christ is present, faith is present. Where Christ is absent, faith is absent.

Kathryn Kuhlman often told the story of Jesus crossing the Sea of Galilee with His disciples in a small boat. A terrific storm arose and the disciples were frightened. . . . They awakened Christ and said, "Master, master, we perish" (Luke 8:24).

Jesus arose and rebuked the wind. The raging waters were suddenly calm. Then He asked the disciples, "Where is your faith?"

After telling the story, Miss Kuhlman asked [this] question about the disciples' faith: "Where was it?" . . .

She concluded, "Their faith had been resting in the stern of the boat! . . . Jesus was their faith."

THIS IS YOUR DAY
FOR A MIRACLE
∽◯

The Miracle of Healing

Be sanctified totally through God's healing Spirit.

Now may the God of peace Himself sanctify you completely; and may your whole spirit, soul, and body be preserved blameless at the coming of our Lord Jesus Christ.

1 THESSALONIANS 5:23

May God's miracle-working power be glorified in you.

We also pray always for you that our God would count you worthy of this calling, and fulfill all the good pleasure of His goodness and the work of faith with power, that the name of our Lord Jesus Christ may be glorified in you, and you in Him, according to the grace of our God and the Lord Jesus Christ.

2 THESSALONIANS 1:11–12

In Christ there is healing comfort.

Now may our Lord Jesus Christ Himself, and our God and Father, who has loved us and given us everlasting consolation and good hope by grace, comfort your hearts and establish you in every good word and work.

2 THESSALONIANS 2:16–17

Benny Hinn

JESUS CHRIST ministered with the power of the Holy Spirit in every miracle that happened in His ministry—from turning water into wine to the cleansing of the ten lepers. Remember, there were no miracles before the Holy Spirit descended on Him at the river Jordan. . . .

The Lord Jesus, filled with God's Spirit, had a specific mission to accomplish. In this first coming He was not to be a conquering king, but rather a gentle lamb.

To multiply the ministry and train His followers, the Lord Jesus sent out seventy of His disciples to heal the sick and preach the Kingdom of God. When they returned and reported that even the demons were subject to them in the name of Jesus, the Savior "rejoiced in the Spirit" (Luke 10:21). The Lord revealed the source and the meaning of this extraordinary power when He said, "If I cast out demons by the Spirit of God, surely the kingdom of God has come upon you" (Matt. 12:28).

WELCOME,
HOLY SPIRIT

The Miracle of Healing

Walk in your healing, flee evil, and fight the good fight of faith.

But you, O man of God, flee these things and pursue righteousness, godliness, faith, love, patience, gentleness. Fight the good fight of faith, lay hold on eternal life, to which you were also called and have confessed the good confession in the presence of many witnesses.

1 TIMOTHY 6:11–12

Rebuke any spirit of fear in your illness.

God has not given us a spirit of fear, but of power and of love and of a sound mind.

2 TIMOTHY 1:7

THE IDEA OF living in a wilderness is not pleasant. It is barren; a place of snakes, scorpions, and death. But the Spirit of the Lord can change the landscape into a garden—a place of beauty and abundance.

As Christians, when we produce a harvest we extol the praises of the Lord. The Master said, "By this My Father is glorified, that you bear much fruit" (John 15:8).

It is the Holy Spirit who enriches our soil and sends the rain in preparation for a thanksgiving feast. He is the one who makes the harvest possible.

It's not your fruit, but His. That is why the Scripture calls it "the fruit of the Spirit." When we present our vessels, He fills them to overflowing.

WELCOME,
HOLY SPIRIT

The Miracle of Healing

Your healing comes from God's mercy.

*Not by works of righteousness which we have done,
but according to His mercy he saved us, through
the washing of regeneration and renewing of the
Holy Spirit.*

TITUS 3:5

Walk in your healing and refresh others.

*We have great joy and consolation in your love,
because the hearts of the saints have been refreshed
by you, brother.*

PHILEMON 7

Benny Hinn

I WANT THOSE of you who have experienced the heartache of a wrenching home situation in your childhood to pay special attention. None of us *come from* perfect homes, and none of us *provide* perfect homes, no matter how hard we try. But perhaps your childhood was characterized by abuse, lack of love, insecurity, or turmoil. And beneath the anger or even the denial are deep feelings of hurt and profound questions about your worth. . . .

Believe me, I can relate to you. I've lived through a war, endured the agony of a transcontinental move, changing languages, schools, friends, countries, and cultures. I've experienced the devastation of parental rejection when I was born again. . . . When Christ found me, I was basically a destroyed person with regard to my self-image, and yet it was at these very points that the Holy Spirit provided such comfort and assurance that I was His— that I actually belonged to Jesus my Savior and God my heavenly Father.

Whatever your background, when you trust Christ, you become a member of the best family there is.

WELCOME,
HOLY SPIRIT

The Miracle of Healing

Be confident of your healing in Christ—don't give up; don't let go.

We have become partakers of Christ if we hold the beginning of our confidence steadfast unto the end.

HEBREWS 3:14

Boldly approach God's throne of grace to seek your healing.

Let us therefore come boldly to the throne of grace, that we may obtain mercy and find grace to help in time of need.

HEBREWS 4:16

Walk in your healing.

Strengthen the hands which hang down, and the feeble knees, and make straight paths for your feet, so that what is lame may not be dislocated, but rather be healed.

HEBREWS 12:13

Benny Hinn

JESUS SAID, "Ask the Father in My name." Even though you are approaching God through His Son, it is still the Father you are asking for the gift. And your request goes *through* the Son to the Father.

How is that gift returned? Let's say your request is for healing. God the Father . . . looks at God the Son and says, "Would you please heal him?"

Christ delivers the healing. Why? Because that is the role of the administrator. The very word *administrate* means to minister or to serve. So the Father releases the healing to the Son, and the Son serves it to you.

Can you picture yourself reaching out to receive your healing and finding that somehow it seems just out of your reach? . . . That's where the work of the Holy Spirit enters the picture. He presents Himself to manifest the healing that was provided by God and served by His Son. *It is the Spirit who completes the process of your healing.*

GOOD MORNING,
HOLY SPIRIT

The Miracle of Healing

Receive the good gift of your healing.

Every good gift and every perfect gift is from above, and comes down from the Father of lights, with whom is no variation or shadow of turning.

JAMES 1:17

Resist the devil's attacks on your health.

Submit to God. Resist the devil and he will flee from you.

JAMES 4:7

Ask the elders to pray for you.

Confess your trespasses to one another, and pray for one another, that you may be healed. The effective, fervent prayer of a righteous man avails much.

JAMES 5:16

ALL THINGS ARE possible
through prayer. . . .

I believe prayer is faith passing into
action. When we pray, all that God
is and has becomes ours. All we
need to do is ask. As the Bible says,
"Ye have not, because ye ask not,"
(James 4:2, KJV). I've heard it said,
"The strongest one in Christ's
kingdom is he who is the best
knocker." So start knocking and
you will find (Luke 11:9–10).

God hears and answers
prayers because the blood of
Jesus has cleansed us of our sins
and provided access to the
throne of God.

Because of Christ's stripes, we can be healed.

Who Himself bore our sins in His own body on the tree, that we, having died to sins, might live for righteousness—by whose stripes you were healed.

1 PETER 2:24

Grace be multiplied to you for your healing.

Grace and peace be multiplied to you in the knowledge of God and of Jesus our Lord, as His divine power has given to us all things that pertain to life and godliness, through the knowledge of Him who called us by glory and virtue.

2 PETER 1:2–3

Repent and claim God's promises of healing.

The Lord is not slack concerning His promise, as some count slackness, but is longsuffering toward us, not willing that any should perish but that all should come to repentance.

2 PETER 3:9

Benny Hinn

I DON'T CARE how hopeless your situation may seem. It's not any worse than the problem Jairus faced (Mark 5:22–43). This man lost his girl, and Jesus said, "Don't be afraid, don't give up. Only believe!" What a powerful word of encouragement!

Jairus must have been elated as life returned to the body of his little daughter. Just moments before, his heart had been pounding with anxiety, grief, and uncertainty. But then Jesus stepped into the midst of Jairus' emotional storm and said, "Don't give up, it's not over yet. I'm still here. Everything is going to be all right!"

You, too, must not give up, because Jesus Christ has won the victory on your behalf as well. And as long as He has won that victory . . . as long as He is the victor . . .what are you worried about?

DON'T GIVE UP!

The Miracle of Healing

Confessing brings cleansing; cleansing brings healing.

If we walk in the light as He is in the light, we have fellowship with one another, and the blood of Jesus Christ His Son cleanses us from all sin. If we say that we have no sin, we deceive ourselves, and the truth is not in us. If we confess our sins, He is faithful and just to forgive us our sins and to cleanse us from all unrighteousness.

1 John 1:7–9

Walking in health means walking in love and obedience.

This is love, that we walk according to His commandments. This is the commandment, that as you have heard from the beginning, you should walk in it.

2 John 1:6

Benny Hinn

THE HOLY SPIRIT is your helper. Yes, He is your assistant to help you receive the life, the healing, or the deliverance you so desperately need.

Often someone asks, "Benny, who should I pray to?" My answer is, "Please don't confuse the issue. You pray to the Father."

Do you know what the meaning of the word *prayer* is? Prayer means petition. In other words you come with your need asking for an answer. You come looking and expecting to receive. You never look to the Spirit—He's the one who *helps* you look.

To this day I have never said, "Holy Spirit, 'give me.'" But I can't count the times I've said, "Precious Holy Spirit, help me ask!"

Are you beginning to realize that your answer is only a breath away? Just a word, waiting to be spoken.

GOOD MORNING,
HOLY SPIRIT

The Miracle of Healing

May you prosper in health.

Beloved, I pray that you may prosper in all things and be in health, just as your soul prospers.

3 JOHN 1:2

God our Savior will keep you from falling.

Now to Him who is able to keep you from stumbling,
And to present you faultless
Before the presence of His glory with exceeding joy,
To God our Savior,
Who alone is wise,
Be glory and majesty,
Dominion and power,
Both now and forever.
Amen.

JUDE 24–25

Benny Hinn

DO YOU KNOW what is greater
than the healing of cancer?
Or greater than commanding
leprosy to be cleansed? Or greater
than commanding the wind to
be calm? The most pivotal miracle
in God's kingdom is the miracle
of salvation. You can tell the world,
"My sins are under the blood.
I have been delivered." . . .

The Lord Jesus could not testify
of His own salvation, for He did
not get saved—He is the Savior.
But you can testify about your
salvation. You can stand and say,
"Once I belonged to Satan,
but now I belong to God the
Father and His Son Jesus Christ.

The Miracle of Healing

There is healing in the Alpha and the Omega.

"I am the Alpha and the Omega, the Beginning and the End," says the Lord, who is and who was and who is to come, the Almighty.

REVELATION 1:8

Eternal healing is your inheritance in Christ.

I heard a loud voice from heaven saying, "Behold, the tabernacle of God is with men, and He will dwell with them, and they shall be His people. God Himself will be with them and be their God. And God will wipe away every tear from their eyes; there shall be no more death, nor sorrow, nor crying. There shall be no more pain, for the former things have passed away."

REVELATION 21:3–4

Pray for the healing of all nations.

In the middle of its street, and on either side of the river, was there the tree of life, which bore twelve fruits, each tree yielding its fruit every month. The leaves of the tree were for the healing of the nations.

REVELATION 22:2

Benny Hinn

YEARS AGO I heard Corrie Ten Boom share a powerful illustration about the timeliness of God's loving care. The setting for the story was Nazi-occupied Holland. . . . In the midst of increasing danger and turmoil she said, "Papa, everything is getting so bad. If the police come for us, how will we know that God is with us?"

"Corrie," he responded, "when we go on a trip by train, when do I give you the ticket?"

"Just before we get on the train, Papa," Corrie answered.

"That's right, Corrie," her father said. "You don't need your ticket until you are about to board the train. . . . That's how our wonderful heavenly Father is. He always gives us just what we need, and He is never late. His love and mercy will sustain us and strengthen us just when we need them, for He is always faithful."

THE BIBLICAL ROAD
TO BLESSING

The Miracle of Healing

Grateful acknowledgment is made to the following publishers and copyright holders for permission to reprint copyrighted material:

Benny Hinn, *The Biblical Road to Blessing.* Nashville, Tn.: Thomas Nelson Publishers, 1997.

Benny Hinn, *The Blood: Its Power from Genesis to Jesus to You.* Orlando, Fl.: Creation House, 1993.

Benny Hinn, *The Day After a Miracle*, Orlando, Fl.: Benny Hinn Media Ministries, 1993.

Benny Hinn, *Don't Give Up!* Orlando, Fl.: Benny Hinn Media Ministries, 1995.

Benny Hinn, *Good Morning, Holy Spirit.* Nashville, Tn.: Thomas Nelson Publishers, 1990.

Benny Hinn, *Healing in Every Book of the Bible.* Benny Hinn Media Ministries, 1998.

Benny Hinn, *The Natural and Spiritual Realms of Healing*, Fl.: Benny Hinn Media Ministries, 1995.

Benny Hinn, *This Is Your Day for a Miracle.* Lake Mary, Fl.: Creation House, 1996.

Benny Hinn, *Welcome, Holy Spirit.* Nashville, Tn.: Thomas Nelson, Publishers, 1995.

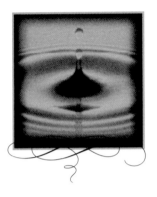

Prayer Requests:

_____

_____

_____

_____

_____

_____

_____

_____

_____

_____

_____

_____

JESUS WENT FROM the throne to the
cross to save us. He went from the cross
to the throne to become our high priest
and enable us to enter God's presence.

Benny Hinn

120

Answers
to Prayer:

_____

_____

_____

_____

_____

_____

_____

_____

_____

_____

_____

_____

_____

_____

_____

_____

_____

_____

_____

_____

_____

_____

_____

The Miracle of Healing

Prayer Requests:

Answers
to Prayer:

_____
_____
_____
_____
_____
_____
_____
_____
_____
_____
_____
_____
_____
_____
_____
_____

EACH DAY IS AN ADVENTURE
as we find our loving heavenly
Father meeting our needs and so
much more in ways that we
would never have anticipated.

The Miracle of Healing

My personal Promises from God's Word

IF THE LORD COULD TURN mud
into man by His breath, think what
He can do by breathing on us again!

Benny Hinn

The Miracle of Healing

My Prayer of Thanksgiving and Praise

_____

_____

_____

_____

_____

_____

_____

_____

_____

_____

_____

_____

_____

_____

_____

Benny Hinn

I PRAY that even at this very
moment faith will arise in your
heart in Jesus' name and that you
will be healed. Even now, receive
the Word of God and be healed
in Jesus' mighty name.

BENNY HINN

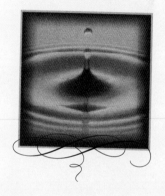

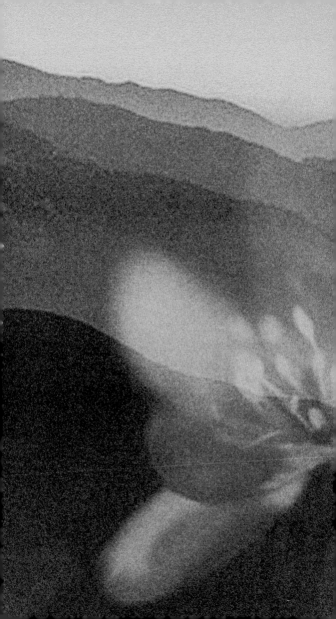